Y²J™

YIELD TO JESUS

*Words of Peace, Wisdom, and Encouragement
for the New Millennium*

Text copyright ©1999
The C. R. Gibson Company
All Rights Reserved
Published by C. R. Gibson ® Norwalk, Connecticut 06856
Created for C. R. Gibson by Matthew A. Price
Cover design by Maria F. Cheek
C. R. Gibson is a registered trademark of Thomas Nelson, Inc.
Printed in the United States of America
ISBN: 0-7667-6183-5

PREFACE

In 1871 an Illinois businessman and attorney named Horatio G. Spafford lost most of his fortune when the great Chicago Fire swept through the city, destroying real estate holdings he had invested in along the shore of Lake Michigan. Two years later, after working tirelessly to rebuild his career and estate, Spafford, his wife, and four daughters decided to take a much needed vacation. A deeply religious family they planned their trip around the speaking tour evangelist Dwight L. Moody had scheduled in Europe during the autumn so they could assist with the crusade.

Because of various commitments Spafford stayed in Chicago while his family sailed to England. His plan was to follow them a few days later. Sadly, the ship his wife and children were on collided with another vessel and sank with most on board. Mrs. Spafford's terse cable to her husband bore the terrible news, "Saved Alone." Spafford embarked immediately to join his bereaved wife. As he passed near the area where his four beloved daughters had drowned he was moved to compose one of the world's best known and most loved hymns, "It Is Well With My Soul." Its opening stanza reads, "When peace, like a river, attendeth my way, When sorrows like sea billows roll— Whatever my lot, Thou hast taught me to say, It is well, it is well with my soul." Despite his grief, Spafford was comforted by the knowledge that God is in control of the lives of his people and that his four little girls were eternally safe in the arms of their Savior.

During times of uncertainty and hardship — from global warfare to economic depressions — the promise that God's love for us is boundless and that, in turn, Christians are to share this love with others has been the foundation upon which believers have built and rebuilt their lives. As we approach the new millennium, many pundits are forecasting the world-wide collapse of all systems and services operated by computer programs that will read the year 2000 as 1900. Yet, regardless of whether these predictions are accurate or not, God promises that if we will only yield our problems and concerns to Him then we, too, will have "peace, like a river." And, not only will this peace quench our own spirit, it will refresh and encourage those around us as well.

*Y**ield to Jesus.* It is sometimes difficult to surrender our fears and concerns to Him but if we do, our doubts will be transformed into courage and we will be able to face what lies ahead. In this little volume you will find words of encouragement from Scripture and from those whose lives are a testimony to God's providence. People like Horatio Spafford who learned to yield his grief to God. His story didn't end that cold day as he stood on deck looking out over the tossing waves. He and his wife later had two more daughters. Together they founded a ministry to the poor in Jerusalem that continues to this day.

WORDS OF
PEACE, WISDOM, AND ENCOURAGEMENT FROM
SCRIPTURE

He will yet fill your mouth with laughing,
and your lips with rejoicing.

Job 8:21

You have put gladness in my heart,
more than in the season that their grain and wine increased.

Psalms 4:7

But let all those rejoice who put their trust in You;
let them ever shout for joy, because You defend them;
let those also who love Your name be joyful in You.

Psalms 5:11

I will be glad and rejoice in You;
I will sing praise to Your name,
O Most High.

Psalms 9:2

But I have trusted in Your mercy;
my heart shall rejoice in Your salvation.

Psalms 13:5

O LORD, You are the portion of my inheritance and my cup;
You maintain my lot.

Psalms 16:5

I have set the LORD always before me;
because He is at my right hand I shall not be moved.
Therefore my heart is glad, and my glory rejoices;
my flesh also will rest in hope.

Psalms 16:8, 9

You will show me the path of life; In Your presence is fullness of joy;
at Your right hand are pleasures forevermore.

Psalms 16:11

As for me, I will see Your face in righteousness;
I shall be satisfied when I awake in Your likeness.

Psalms 17:15

The law of the LORD is perfect, converting the soul;
the testimony of the LORD is sure, making wise the simple.

Psalms 19:7, 8

For You have made him most blessed forever;
You have made him exceedingly glad with Your presence.

Psalms 21:6

The LORD is my strength and my shield;
my heart trusted in Him, and I am helped;
therefore my heart greatly rejoices,
and with my song I will praise Him.

Psalms 28:7

For His anger is but for a moment, His favor is for life;
weeping may endure for a night, but joy comes in the morning.

Psalms 30:5

You have turned for me my mourning into dancing;
You have put off my sackcloth and clothed me with gladness.

Psalms 30:11

The young lions lack and suffer hunger;
but those who seek the LORD shall not lack any good thing.

Psalms 34:10

And my soul shall be joyful in the LORD; it shall rejoice in His salvation.

Psalms 35:9

Let all those who seek You rejoice and be glad in You; let such as love
Your salvation say continually, "The LORD be magnified!"

Psalms 40:16

Cast your burden on the LORD, and He shall sustain you;
He shall never permit the righteous to be moved.

Psalms 55:22

The humble shall see this and be glad; and you who seek God,
your hearts shall live.

Psalms 69:32

For the LORD God is a sun and shield; the LORD will give grace and
glory; no good thing will He withhold from those who walk uprightly.

Psalms 84:11

Those who sow in tears shall reap in joy.
Psalms 126:5

The LORD will perfect that which concerns me;
Your mercy, O LORD, endures forever;
do not forsake the works of Your hands.

Psalms 138:8

Who made heaven and earth, the sea, and all that is in them;
who keeps truth forever, who executes justice for the oppressed,
who gives food to the hungry. The LORD gives freedom to the prisoners.
The LORD opens the eyes of the blind; the LORD raises those who are
bowed down; the LORD loves the righteous. The LORD watches over
the strangers; He relieves the fatherless and widows.

Psalms 146:6-9a

He stores up sound wisdom for the upright;
He is a shield to those who walk uprightly;
He guards the paths of justice, and preserves the way of His saints.

Proverbs 2:7, 8

Let not mercy and truth forsake you; bind them around your neck,
write them on the tablet of your heart,
and so find favor and high esteem in the sight of God and man.

Proverbs 3:3, 4

Do not be wise in your own eyes; fear the LORD and depart from evil.
It will be health to your flesh, and strength to your bones.
Honor the LORD with your possessions, and with the firstfruits of all
your increase; so your barns will be filled with plenty,
and your vats will overflow with new wine.

Proverbs 3:710

Happy is the man who finds wisdom, and the man who gains
understanding; for her proceeds are better than the profits of silver,
and her gain than fine gold. She is more precious than rubies,
and all the things you may desire cannot compare with her.
Length of days is in her right hand, in her left hand riches and honor.
Her ways are ways of pleasantness, and all her paths are peace.
She is a tree of life to those who take hold of her,
and happy are all who retain her.

Proverbs 3:1318

The hope of the righteous will be gladness,
but the expectation of the wicked will perish.

Proverbs 10:28

The fear of the LORD leads to life,
and he who has it will abide in satisfaction;
he will not be visited with evil.

Proverbs 19:23

For God gives wisdom and knowledge and joy
to a man who is good in His sight.

Ecclesiastes 2:26a

Words of Peace, Wisdom, and *Encouragement from Scripture*

To everything there is a season, a time for every purpose
under heaven: A time to be born, and a time to die;
a time to plant, and a time to pluck what is planted;
a time to kill, and a time to heal; a time to break down,
and a time to build up; a time to weep, and a time to laugh;
a time to mourn, and a time to dance; a time to cast away stones,
and a time to gather stones; a time to embrace,
and a time to refrain from embracing; a time to gain,
and a time to lose; a time to keep, and a time to throw away;
a time to tear, and a time to sew; a time to keep silence,
and a time to speak; a time to love, and a time to hate;
a time of war, and a time of peace.

Ecclesiastes 3:1-8

I know that whatever God does, it shall be forever.
Nothing can be added to it, and nothing taken from it.
Ecclesiastes 3:14a

Two are better than one, because they have a good reward
for their labor. For if they fall, one will lift up his companion.
Ecclesiastes 4:9, 10a

Do not say, "Why were the former days better than these?"
for you do not inquire wisely concerning this.
Ecclesiastes 7:10

For wisdom is a defense as money is a defense,
but the excellence of knowledge is that wisdom gives life
to those who have it.

Ecclesiastes 7:12

In the day of prosperity be joyful,
but in the day of adversity consider:
Surely God has appointed the one as well as the other,
so that man can find out nothing that will come after him.

Ecclesiastes 7:14

Who is like a wise man?
And who knows the interpretation of a thing?
A man's wisdom makes his face shine,
and the sternness of his face is changed.

Ecclesiastes 8:1

For he does not know what will happen;
so who can tell him when it will occur?

Ecclesiastes 8:7

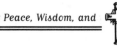

I returned and saw under the sun that; the race is not to the swift,
nor the battle to the strong, nor bread to the wise,
nor riches to men of understanding, nor favor to men of skill;
but time and chance happen to them all.

Ecclesiastes 9:11

Because of laziness the building decays,
and through idleness of hands the house leaks.

Ecclesiastes 10:18

As you do not know what is the way of the wind,
or how the bones grow in the womb of her who is with child,
so you do not know the works of God who makes everything.
In the morning sow your seed, and in the evening do not withhold
your hand; for you do not know which will prosper,
either this or that, or whether both alike will be good.

Ecclesiastes 11:5, 6

Remember now your Creator in the days of your youth,
before the difficult days come, and the years draw near when you say,
"I have no pleasure in them.

Ecclesiastes 12:1

Behold, God is my salvation, I will trust and not be afraid;
For the LORD is my strength and song; He also has become my salvation.
Therefore with joy you will draw water from the wells of salvation.

Isaiah 12:2, 3

O LORD, You are my God. I will exalt You, I will praise Your name,
for You have done wonderful things;
Your counsels of old are faithfulness and truth.

Isaiah 25:1

You will keep him in perfect peace, whose mind is stayed on You,
because he trusts in You. Trust in the LORD forever,
For in YAHWEH, the LORD, is everlasting strength.

Isaiah 26:3, 4

The way of the just is uprightness; O Most Upright,
You weigh the path of the just.

Isaiah 26:7

LORD, You will establish peace for us,
for You have also done all our works in us.

Isaiah 26:12

Therefore the LORD will wait, that He may be gracious to you;
and therefore He will be exalted, that He may have mercy on you.
For the LORD is a God of justice;
blessed are all those who wait for Him.

Isaiah 30:18

The work of righteousness will be peace,
and the effect of righteousness, quietness and assurance forever.
My people will dwell in a peaceful habitation,
in secure dwellings, and in quiet resting places.

Isaiah 32:17, 18

Every valley shall be exalted and every mountain and hill brought low;
the crooked places shall be made straight and the rough places smooth;
the glory of the LORD shall be revealed,
and all flesh shall see it together; for the mouth of the LORD has spoken.

Isaiah 40:4, 5

The grass withers, the flower fades,
but the word of our God stands forever.

Isaiah 40:8

Those who wait on the LORD shall renew their strength;
they shall mount up with wings like eagles,
they shall run and not be weary, they shall walk and not faint.

Isaiah 40:31

Fear not, for I am with you; be not dismayed, for I am your God.
I will strengthen you, yes, I will help you,
I will uphold you with My righteous right hand.

Isaiah 41:10

For I will pour water on him who is thirsty,
and floods on the dry ground; I will pour My Spirit on your descendants,
and My blessing on your offspring.

Isaiah 44:3

How beautiful upon the mountains are the feet of him who brings
good news, who proclaims peace, who brings glad tidings of good
things, who proclaims salvation, who says to Zion, "Your God reigns!"

Isaiah 52:7

Seek the LORD while He may be found,
call upon Him while He is near.

Isaiah 55:6

For you shall go out with joy, and be led out with peace;
the mountains and the hills shall break forth into singing before you,
and all the trees of the field shall clap their hands.

Isaiah 55:12

Thus says the LORD: "Keep justice, and do righteousness, for
My salvation is about to come, and My righteousness to be revealed."

Isaiah 56:1

If you turn away your foot from the Sabbath, from doing
your pleasure on My holy day, and call the Sabbath a delight,
the holy day of the LORD honorable, and shall honor Him,
not doing your own ways, nor finding your own pleasure,
nor speaking your own words, then you shall delight yourself in the
LORD; and I will cause you to ride on the high hills of the earth,
and feed you with the heritage of Jacob your father.
The mouth of the LORD has spoken.

Isaiah 58:13, 14

For behold, I create new heavens and a new earth;
and the former shall not be remembered or come to mind.

Isaiah 65:17

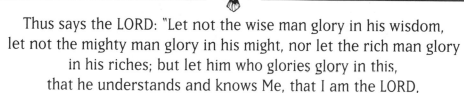

Thus says the LORD: "Let not the wise man glory in his wisdom,
let not the mighty man glory in his might, nor let the rich man glory
in his riches; but let him who glories glory in this,
that he understands and knows Me, that I am the LORD,
exercising loving kindness, judgment, and righteousness in the earth.
For in these I delight," says the LORD.

Jeremiah 9:23, 24

Blessed is the man who trusts in the LORD,
and whose hope is the LORD. For he shall be like a tree
planted by the waters, which spreads out its roots by the river,
and will not fear when heat comes; but its leaf will be green,
and will not be anxious in the year of drought,
nor will cease from yielding fruit.

Jeremiah 17:7, 8

Yes, I have loved you with an everlasting love;
therefore with lovingkindness I have drawn you.

Jeremiah 31:3b

And He changes the times and the seasons;
He removes kings and raises up kings; He gives wisdom to the wise
and knowledge to those who have understanding.

Daniel 2:21

Let us know, let us pursue the knowledge of the LORD.
His going forth is established as the morning;
He will come to us like the rain,
like the latter and former rain to the earth.

Hosea 6:3

And it shall come to pass afterward that I will pour out My Spirit
on all flesh; your sons and your daughters shall prophesy,
your old men shall dream dreams, your young men shall see visions.

Joel 2:28

The LORD your God in your midst, the Mighty One, will save;
He will rejoice over you with gladness,
He will quiet you with His love,
He will rejoice over you with singing.

Zephaniah 3:17

Therefore you now have sorrow; but I will see you again
and your heart will rejoice, and your joy no one will take from you.
And in that day you will ask Me nothing. Most assuredly, I say to you,
whatever you ask the Father in My name He will give you.
Until now you have asked nothing in My name.
Ask, and you will receive, that your joy may be full.

John 16:22-24

These things I have spoken to you, that in Me you may have peace.
In the world you will have tribulation; but be of good cheer,
I have overcome the world.

John 16:33

For not the hearers of the law are just in the sight of God,
but the doers of the law will be justified.

Romans 2:13

Therefore, having been justified by faith,
we have peace with God through our Lord Jesus Christ,
through whom also we have access by faith into this grace
in which we stand, and rejoice in hope of the glory of God.

Romans 5:1, 2

But God demonstrates His own love toward us,
in that while we were still sinners, Christ died for us.

Romans 5:8

For I consider that the sufferings of this present time are not worthy
to be compared with the glory which shall be revealed in us.

Romans 8:18

And we know that all things work together for good to those
who love God, to those who are the called according to His purpose.

Romans 8:28

For I am persuaded that neither death nor life,
nor angels nor principalities nor powers, nor things present
nor things to come, nor height nor depth,
nor any other created thing, shall be able to separate us from
the love of God which is in Christ Jesus our Lord.

Romans 8:38, 39

And do not be conformed to this world, but be transformed
by the renewing of your mind, that you may prove
what is that good and acceptable and perfect will of God.

Romans 12:2

Be kindly affectionate to one another with brotherly love,
in honor giving preference to one another; not lagging in diligence,
fervent in spirit, serving the Lord; rejoicing in hope,
patient in tribulation, continuing steadfastly in prayer;
distributing to the needs of the saints, given to hospitality.

Romans 12:10-13

Rejoice with those who rejoice, and weep with those who weep.
Be of the same mind toward one another. Do not set your mind
on high things, but associate with the humble.
Do not be wise in your own opinion.

Romans 12:15, 16

Owe no one anything except to love one another,
for he who loves another has fulfilled the law.

Romans 13:8

For if we live, we live to the Lord; and if we die, we die to the Lord.
Therefore, whether we live or die, we are the Lord's.

Romans 14:8

The foolishness of God is wiser than men,
and the weakness of God is stronger than men.

1 Corinthians 1:25

Do you not know that you are the temple of God
and that the Spirit of God dwells in you?

1 Corinthians 3:16

Therefore, whether you eat or drink, or whatever you do,
do all to the glory of God.

1 Corinthians 10:31

Though I speak with the tongues of men and of angels,
but have not love, I have become sounding brass or a clanging cymbal.
And though I have the gift of prophecy, and understand all mysteries
and all knowledge, and though I have all faith,
so that I could remove mountains, but have not love, I am nothing.
And though I bestow all my goods to feed the poor, and though I give
my body to be burned, but have not love, it profits me nothing.
Love suffers long and is kind; love does not envy;
love does not parade itself, is not puffed up; does not behave rudely,
does not seek its own, is not provoked, thinks no evil;
does not rejoice in iniquity, but rejoices in the truth; bears all things,
believes all things, hopes all things, endures all things.

1 Corinthians 13:1-7

And now abide faith, hope, love, these three;
but the greatest of these is love.
1 Corinthians 13:13

For God is not the author of confusion but of peace.
1 Corinthians 14:33a

Therefore, my beloved brethren, be steadfast, immovable,
always abounding in the work of the Lord,
knowing that your labor is not in vain in the Lord.
1 Corinthians 15:58

Watch, stand fast in the faith, be brave, be strong.
Let all that you do be done with love.

1 Corinthians 16:13, 14

For our light affliction, which is but for a moment,
is working for us a far more exceeding and eternal weight of glory,
while we do not look at the things which are seen,
but at the things which are not seen.
For the things which are seen are temporary,
but the things which are not seen are eternal.

2 Corinthians 4:17, 18

For we walk by faith, not by sight.

2 Corinthians 5:7

Therefore, if anyone is in Christ, he is a new creation;
old things have passed away; behold, all things have become new.

2 Corinthians 5:17

And God is able to make all grace abound toward you, that you,
always having all sufficiency in all things,
may have an abundance for every good work.

2 Corinthians 9:8

Concerning this thing I pleaded with the Lord three times that it might depart from me. And He said to me, "My grace is sufficient for you, for My strength is made perfect in weakness."
Therefore most gladly I will rather boast in my infirmities, that the power of Christ may rest upon me. Therefore I take pleasure in infirmities, in reproaches, in needs, in persecutions, in distresses, for Christ's sake. For when I am weak, then I am strong.

2 Corinthians 12:810

But the fruit of the Spirit is love, joy, peace, longsuffering, kindness, goodness, faithfulness, gentleness, selfcontrol.
Against such there is no law.

Galatians 5:22, 23

Bear one another's burdens, and so fulfill the law of Christ.

Galatians 6:2

And let us not grow weary while doing good,
for in due season we shall reap if we do not lose heart.

Galatians 6:9

For we are His workmanship, created in Christ Jesus for good works,
which God prepared beforehand that we should walk in them.

Ephesians 2:10

Now to Him who is able to do exceedingly abundantly
above all that we ask or think, according to the power that works in us,
to Him be glory in the church by Christ Jesus to all generations,
forever and ever. Amen.

Ephesians 3:20, 21

And be kind to one another, tenderhearted, forgiving one another,
just as God in Christ forgave you.

Ephesians 4:32

Therefore be imitators of God as dear children. And walk in love, as
Christ also has loved us and given Himself for us, an offering and a
sacrifice to God for a sweet smelling aroma.

Ephesians 5:1, 2

See then that you walk circumspectly, not as fools but as wise,
redeeming the time, because the days are evil.

Ephesians 5:15, 16

Be filled with the Spirit, speaking to one another in psalms and hymns
and spiritual songs, singing and making melody in your heart
to the Lord, giving thanks always for all things to God the Father
in the name of our Lord Jesus Christ.

Ephesians 5:18b-20

Put on the whole armor of God,
that you may be able to stand against the wiles of the devil.
Ephesians 6:11

And take the helmet of salvation, and the sword of the Spirit,
which is the word of God; praying always with all prayer and
supplication in the Spirit, being watchful to this end
with all perseverance and supplication for all the saints.
Ephesians 6:17, 18

Do all things without complaining and disputing,
that you may become blameless and harmless, children of God
without fault in the midst of a crooked and perverse generation,
among whom you shine as lights in the world.

Philippians 2:14, 15

For our citizenship is in heaven, from which we also eagerly wait
for the Savior, the Lord Jesus Christ, who will transform
our lowly body that it may be conformed to His glorious body,
according to the working by which He is able even to subdue
all things to Himself.

Philippians 3:20, 21

Rejoice in the Lord always. Again I will say, rejoice!
Let your gentleness be known to all men. The Lord is at hand.
Be anxious for nothing, but in everything by prayer and supplication,
with thanksgiving, let your requests be made known to God;
and the peace of God, which surpasses all understanding,
will guard your hearts and minds through Christ Jesus.
Finally, brethren, whatever things are true,
whatever things are noble, whatever things are just,
whatever things are pure, whatever things are lovely,
whatever things are of good report, if there is any virtue
and if there is anything praiseworthy; meditate on these things.
Philippians 4:4-8

And my God shall supply all your need according to His riches
in glory by Christ Jesus.
Philippians 4:19

Set your mind on things above,
not on things on the earth.
Colossians 3:2

Therefore, as the elect of God, holy and beloved,
put on tender mercies, kindness, humility, meekness, longsuffering;
bearing with one another, and forgiving one another,
if anyone has a complaint against another; even as Christ forgave you,
so you also must do. But above all these things put on love,
which is the bond of perfection. And let the peace of God rule
in your hearts, to which also you were called in one body;
and be thankful. Let the word of Christ dwell in you richly
in all wisdom, teaching and admonishing one another in psalms and
hymns and spiritual songs, singing with grace in your hearts
to the Lord. And whatever you do in word or deed,
do all in the name of the Lord Jesus,
giving thanks to God the Father through Him.

Colossians 3:12-17

And whatever you do, do it heartily, as to the Lord and not to men,
knowing that from the Lord you will receive
the reward of the inheritance; for you serve the Lord Christ.

Colossians 3:23, 24

Continue earnestly in prayer, being vigilant in it with thanksgiving.

Colossians 4:2

Aspire to lead a quiet life, to mind your own business, and to work
with your own hands, as we commanded you, that you may walk
properly toward those who are outside, and that you may lack nothing.

1 Thessalonians 4:11, 12

Rejoice always, pray without ceasing, in everything give thanks;
for this is the will of God in Christ Jesus for you.
1 Thessalonians 5:16–18

Take heed to yourself and to the doctrine. Continue in them,
for in doing this you will save both yourself and those who hear you.
1 Timothy 4:16

Now godliness with contentment is great gain.
1 Timothy 6:6

Command those who are rich in this present age not to be haughty,
nor to trust in uncertain riches but in the living God,
who gives us richly all things to enjoy.

1 Timothy 6:17

For we have become partakers of Christ
if we hold the beginning of our confidence steadfast to the end.

Hebrews 3:14

His divine power has given to us all things
that pertain to life and godliness, through the knowledge of Him
who called us by glory and virtue.

2 Peter 1:3

Now to Him who is able to keep you from stumbling,
and to present you faultless before the presence of His glory
with exceeding joy, to God our Savior, who alone is wise,
be glory and majesty, dominion and power,
both now and forever. Amen.

Jude 1:24, 25

WORDS OF
PEACE, WISDOM, AND ENCOURAGEMENT FROM
TIMELESS HYMNS

Trusting him while life shall last, Trusting him till earth be past;
Till within the jasper wall, Trusting Jesus, that is all.

"TRUSTING JESUS"

Edgar Page Stites, 1876

I have a home prepared for me, Since I have been redeemed,
Where I shall dwell eternally, Since I have been redeemed.

"SINCE I HAVE BEEN REDEEMED"

Edwin O. Excell, 1884

I know I shall see in his beauty,
The King in whose law I delight;
Who lovingly guardeth my footsteps,
And giveth me songs in the night.
"REDEEMED, HOW I LOVE TO PROCLAIM IT"
Fanny J. Crosby, 1882

O there's sunshine, blessed sunshine,
When the peaceful, happy moments roll;
When Jesus shows his smiling face,
There is sunshine in my soul.
"SUNSHINE IN MY SOUL"
Eliza E. Hewitt, 1887

His word will stand forever, ever;
His truth — it shall be my shield and buckler,
So I'm not afraid.
"I Will Not Be Afraid"
Anonymous

Come to this fountain so rich and sweet,
Cast thy poor soul at the Savior's feet;
Plunge in today, and be made complete;
Glory to his name.
"Down at the Cross"
Elisha A. Hoffman, 1878

Praise in the common things of life,
Its goings out and in;
Praise in each duty and each deed,
However small and mean.
"FILL THOU MY LIFE, O LORD MY GOD"
Horatius Bonar, 1866

How sweet the name of Jesus sounds,
In a believer's ear!
It soothes sorrows, heals his wounds,
And drives away his fear.
"HOW SWEET THE NAME OF JESUS SOUNDS"
John Newton, 1779

In his boundless love and mercy, He the ransom freely gave.
"I WILL SING OF MY REDEEMER"
Philip P. Bliss, 1876

Take the name of Jesus ever,
As a shield from ev'ry snare;
When temptations round you gather,
Breathe that holy name in pray'r.
"TAKE THE NAME OF JESUS WITH YOU"
Lydia Baxter, 1870

Was e'er a gift like the Savior given?
No, not one! No, not one!
Will he refuse us a home in heaven?
No, not one! No, no not one!

"No, Not One"

Johnson Oatman, Jr., 1895

When we all get to heaven,
What a day of rejoicing that will be!
When we all see Jesus,
We'll sing and shout the victory.

"When We All Get to Heaven"

Eliza E. Hewitt, 1898

There's a land that is fairer than day,
And by faith we can see it afar;
For the Father waits over the way,
To prepare us a dwelling place there.
"There's a Land That I Fairer than Day"
Sanford F. Bennett, 1868

From him who loves me now so well,
What pow'r my soul can sever?
Shall life or death or earth or hell?
No; I am his forever.
"I've Found a Friend, O Such a Friend"
James G. Small, 1863

He sends the sunshine and the rain,
He sends the harvest's golden grain;
Sunshine and rain, harvest of grain,
He's my friend.

"Jesus Is All the World to Me"

Will L. Thompson, 1904

All my hopes in thee abide,
Thou my hope, and naught beside:
Ever let my glory be,
Only, only, only Thee.

"Blessed Savior, Thee I Love"

George Duffield, Jr., 1851

There is never a day so dreary,
There is never a night so long,
But the soul that is trusting Jesus,
Will somewhere find a song.

"WONDERFUL, WONDERFUL JESUS"

Anna B. Russell, 1921

He lives to bless me with his love,
Glory, hallelujah!
He lives to plead for me above,
Glory, hallelujah!

"I KNOW THAT MY REDEEMER LIVES"

Samuel Medley, 1775

When we walk with the Lord,
In the light of his Word,
What a glory he sheds on our way!
"WHEN WE WALK WITH THE LORD"
John H. Sammis, 1887

And when we arrive at the haven of rest,
We shall hear the glad words,
"Come up hither, you blest,
Here are regions of light, here are mansions of bliss."
O who would not climb such a ladder as this?
"AS JACOB WITH TRAVEL"
Anonymous Folk Hymn

Like a mighty army, Moves the church of God;
Brothers we are treading, Where the saints have trod;
We are not divided; All one body we,
One in hope and doctrine, One in charity.

"ONWARD, CHRISTIAN SOLDIERS"
Sabine Baring-Gould, 1864

Run thou the race thro' God's good grace,
Lift up thine eyes, and seek his face;
Life with its way before us lies,
Christ is the path, and Christ the prize.

"FIGHT THE GOOD FIGHT"
John S.B. Monsell, 1863

Are you weary, are you heavy hearted?
Tell it to Jesus, Tell it to Jesus;
Are you grieving over joys departed?
Tell it to Jesus alone.

"Tell It to Jesus"
Jeremiah E. Rankin, 1888

In seasons of distress and grief,
My soul has often found relief,
And oft escaped the tempter's snare,
By thy return, sweet hour of prayer.

"Sweet Hour of Prayer"
William Walford, 1840

He's a Shepherd, kind and gracious,
And his pastures are delicious;
Constant love to me he shows,
Yea, my very name he knows.

"JESUS MAKES MY HEART REJOICE"
Henriette Luise von Hayn, 1778

Never a trial that he is not there,
Never a burden that he doth not bear,
Never a sorrow that he doth not share,
Moment by moment, I'm under his care.

"MOMENT BY MOMENT"
Daniel W. Whittle, 1893

Faith is the victory, we know, That overcomes the world.

"FAITH IS THE VICTORY"

John H. Yates, 1891

I need thee ev'ry hour, Stay thou near by;
Temptations lose their pow'r, When thou art nigh.

"I NEED THEE EVERY HOUR"

Annie S. Hawks, 1872

Jesus calls us from the worship,
Of the vain world's golden store,
From each idol that would keep us,
Saying, "Christian, love me more."
"Jesus Calls Us o'er the Tumult"
Cecil Frances Alexander, 1852

He will give me grace and glory,
And go with me, with me all the way.
"Where He Leads Me"
E.W. Blandy, 1890

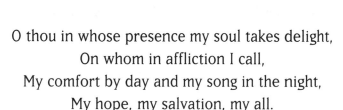

O thou in whose presence my soul takes delight,
On whom in affliction I call,
My comfort by day and my song in the night,
My hope, my salvation, my all.
"O Thou, in Whose Presence"
Frances R. Havergal, 1874

'Tis so sweet to trust in Jesus, Just to take him at his word;
Just to rest upon his promise, Just to know, "Thus saith the Lord."
"'Tis So Sweet to Trust in Jesus"
Louisa M.R. Stead, 1882

There are heights of joy that I may not reach,
Till I rest in peace with thee.
"I Am Thine, O Lord"
Fanny J. Crosby, 1875

O Jesus, thou hast promised, To all who follow thee,
That where thou art in glory, There shall thy servant be.
"O Jesus, I Have Promised"
John E. Bode, 1868

We walk by faith and not by sight.
"We Walk By Faith and Not By Sight"
Henry Alford, 1844

There is a place of full release,
Near to the heart of God,
A place where all is joy and peace,
Near to the heart of God.
"Near to the Heart of God"
Cleland B. McAfee, 1901

Immortal Love, forever full, Forever flowing free,
Forever shared, forever whole, A never ebbing sea!
"Immortal Love, Forever Full"
John Greenleaf Whittier, 1866

Jesus loves me! this I know, For the Bible tells me so;
Little ones to him belong; They are weak, but he is strong.

"Jesus Loves Me"

Anna B. Warner, 1860

Praise God, from whom all blessings flow;
Praise him, all creatures here below;
Praise him above, ye heav'nly host;
Praise Father, Son, and Holy Ghost.

"Praise God from Whom All Blessings Flow"

Thomas Ken, 1695

Blessed assurance, Jesus is mine!
Oh, what a foretaste of glory divine!
"BLESSED ASSURANCE, JESUS IS MINE"
Fanny J. Crosby, 1873

My hope is built on nothing less,
Than Jesus' blood and righteousness;
I dare not trust the sweetest frame,
But wholly lean on Jesus' name.
"THE SOLID ROCK"
Edward Mote, 1832

WORDS OF
PEACE, WISDOM, AND ENCOURAGEMENT FROM
FELLOW BELIEVERS

Yielding to Christ is confessing every known sin in your life,
yielding every area of your life. It means yielding your girl friend,
your boy friend, your family, your business, your career,
your ambitions, your soul, the innermost thoughts and depths
of your heart; yielding them all to Christ, holding nothing back.
Billy Graham

Anxiety is a word of unbelief or unreasoning dread.
We have no right to allow it. Full faith in God puts it to rest.
Horace Bushnell

Sufficient to each day are the duties to be done and the trials to be endured. God never built a Christian strong enough to carry today's duties and tomorrow's anxieties piled on the top of them.

Theodore L. Cuyler

To receive Christ's help, we must wait upon him.

John Owen

Expect great things from God; attempt great things for God.

William Carey

If God remembers the creeping and crawling things
that obey His laws and calls them to another world
after they have finished their life in the pool,
surely He will remember His children who love and serve Him
and call them to a world more beautiful and wonderful
than this when they finish their life here on earth.

R. Albert Goodwin

There is nothing better than peace,
by which all strife in heaven and earth is done away.

Ignatius of Antioch

The hope of the world is in the hands
of those who will not take counsel of despair.

Joseph R. Sizoo

God never permits an evil without good coming from it.

Fulton J. Sheen

The study of God's Word, for the purpose of discovering God's will,
is the secret discipline which has formed the greatest characters.
James W. Alexander

Do you ever sit down and wonder what is wrong with the world?
Do you ever ask yourself why it is that Christians seem to have
so little influence, why they seem to achieve so little,
for all their numbers, in putting the world right?
To each of those two questions there is ultimately but one answer.
It is this: we lack the mind of Christ.
J. Arthur Lewis

If you want not to take your character from your environment
but to put character into it, you will need to draw on spiritual
resources greater than your own. And you may.
You can be strengthened by God in your inner life
if you will open it daily to His influence. It was of this Paul was
thinking when he said: "Be not conformed to this world but be ye
transformed by the renewing of your mind."

Robert James McCracken

Lovely flowers are the smiles of God's goodness.
William Wilberforce

Life, if properly viewed in any aspect, is great,
but mainly great when viewed in its relation to the world to come.

Albert Barnes

We are immortal until our work on earth is done.

George Whitefield

The steady discipline of intimate friendship with Jesus
results in men becoming like Him.

Harry Emerson Fosdick

To saints their very slumber is a prayer.
St. Jerome

Better to fail here (as fail we must) than not to try;
for failure may bring us to a deeper understanding.
George A. Buttrick

An undivided heart which worships God alone,
and trusts him as it should, is raised above anxiety for earthly wants.
Cunningham Geikie

Religion is the fear and love of God; its demonstration is good works; and faith is the root of both, for without faith we cannot please God; nor can we fear and love what we do not believe.

William Penn

Men ask for excitement, when they need enthusiasm.
They ask for solace, when they need salvation.
They seek the sensual, when they need the spiritual.
Everywhere men are asking for goods, when they need God.
Yet the cry comes out of a need that is profound.
The trouble is that men do not understand their own need.

G. Campbell Morgan

One's life is his capital, not his circumstances.

James I. Vance

How fast we learn in a day of sorrow! Scripture shines out in
a new effulgence; every verse seems to contain a sunbeam,
every promise stands out in illuminated splendor;
things hard to be understood become in a moment plain.

Horatius Bonar

Information alone will not change your life.
Revelation in your spirit is what produces change. In fact, that is how
a friend of mine differentiates between information and revelation.
He says, "When you have revelation in your spirit,
there will be immediate change."

Don Crossland

The body of our prayer is the sum of our duty;
and as we must ask of God whatsoever we need,
so we must watch and labor for all that we ask.

Jeremy Taylor

So when our minds are so distracted and our thoughts become
muddied and muddled, we can look up to Christ and rise into a
high mindedness where little things and petty puzzlements
do not reach us.

Ralph W. Sockman

God sometimes washes the eyes of his children with tears
that they may read aright his providence and his commandments.

Theodore L. Cuyler

If the prayer of one or two has great avail,
how much more that of the total Church.

Ignatius of Antioch

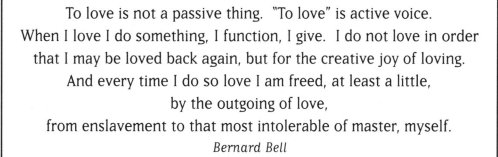

To love is not a passive thing. "To love" is active voice.
When I love I do something, I function, I give. I do not love in order
that I may be loved back again, but for the creative joy of loving.
And every time I do so love I am freed, at least a little,
by the outgoing of love,
from enslavement to that most intolerable of master, myself.

Bernard Bell

All that I am I owe to Jesus Christ,
revealed to me in His divine Book.

David Livingstone

Anyone who is to find Christ must first find the church.
How could anyone know where Christ is and what faith in him is
unless he knew where his believers are?
Martin Luther

What is the chief end of man? You know the answer.
The chief end of man is to glorify God and to enjoy Him forever.
Christ gives us peace with joy. It is the purpose of God in Christ that
the deepest desires of the human heart should be forever satisfied.
Russell Cartwright Stroup

When I was young, I was sure of many things; now there are only two
things of which I am sure: one is, that I am a miserable sinner;
and the other, that Christ is an allsufficient Saviour.
He is well taught who learns these two lessons.
John Newton

It is only Christianity, the great bond of love and duty to God,
that makes any existence valuable or even tolerable.
Horace Bushnell

I was baptized with the Holy Spirit when I took Him by simple faith
in the Word of God.
R.A. Torrey

A loving trust in the Author of the Bible is the best preparation for
a wise and profitable study of the Bible itself.
Henry Clay Trumbell

If every church in our land today could boast that in its gatherings
Christ is king and its people ready, having heard the voice of Christ,
to go to work democratically to do his will, what a Church,
what a land, we should have!
Douglas Horton

Nobody ever outgrows Scripture;
the book widens and deepens with our years.
Charles Haddon Spurgeon

The minority with a mission must bow again before the Master,
and moving out with a message incarnate, certain of life everlasting,
take up the Cross anew, risk all, and thus save all.

John F. Cronin

To holy people the very name of Jesus is a name to feed upon,
a name to transport. His name can raise the dead
and transfigure and beautify the living.

John Henry Newman

No one can save all people, but each of us can save some people.

Harry V. Richardson

The joy of unselfish love is the purest joy that man can taste;
the joy of perfect self-sacrifice is the highest joy that humanity
can possess; and they lie open for us all.

Alexander MacLaren

God wills that all men might be saved. But it is necessary that
they cooperate in this, that they consent to this,
that they do not refuse his Grace, which calls them.

Michel Riquet

If a man cannot be a Christian in the place he is,
he cannot be a Christian anywhere.

Henry Ward Beecher

We have seen that the cross was necessary to break the power of sin
and that it was inescapable even for the Son of God.
But we must not fail to apprehend its personal implications
for ourselves. To believe on Christ, to accept him as
one's personal Savior and Lord, is to die to self and live for God
regardless of the consequences.

Walter N. Roberts

For health and the constant enjoyment of life,
give me a keen and ever present sense of humor;
it is the next best thing to an abiding faith in providence.

George B. Cheever

We are certain that there is forgiveness, because there is a Gospel,
and the very essence of the Gospel lies in
the proclamation of the pardon of sin.

Charles Haddon Spurgeon

Today we live, move, and have our being in the abdomen of God.
We live and move and have our being in God even though we cannot
see the face of God. Now the baby, having made these observations,
may think, "Oh, I am indeed a great philosopher."
But we know that baby is very presumptuous. So with us.
As long as we remain materialistically minded, we are like that baby
—very presumptuous.

Toyohiko Kagawa

The fullest Christian experience is simply the fullest life.

Phillips Brooks

Only out of struggle and pain can there come the kind of person and
the kind of world that the wisdom and power and goodness of God
are set to make. How could you teach any man courage
if there were no fears to fight, no threats to overcome?

Herbert Welch

The Christian needs a reminder every hour; some defeat, surprise,
adversity, peril; to be agitated, mortified, beaten out of his course,
so that all remains of self will be sifted out.

Horace Bushnell

It's not the rules and regulations you follow carefully that will win you favor with God but rather offering your life to Him in complete faith that His Son, Jesus Christ, conquered sin and death on your behalf and for your salvation.

James L. Mathews

God is like the sun at high noon, always giving all he has.

Arthur John Gossip

As the print of the seal on the wax is the express image of the seal itself, so Christ is the express image, the perfect representation, of God.

Ambrose of Milan

'Tis not for man to trifle; life is brief, and sin is here.
We have no time to sport away the hours;
all must be earnest in a world like ours.

Horatius Bonar

The greatest negative in the universe is the Cross, for with it God
wiped out everything that was not of himself; the greatest positive
in the universe is the resurrection, for through it
God brought into being all he will have in the new creation.

Watchman Nee

Try to gather together more frequently to celebrate God's Eucharist
and to praise him. For when you meet with frequency,
Satan's powers are overthrown and his destructiveness is undone
by the unanimity of your faith.

Ignatius of Antioch

When you are tempted to do wrong ask the Savior to help you.
Seek His grace, His strength, His blessing in everything you do.
Let His love control all your thoughts and actions. America needs
more boys and girls, more men and women whose hearts are great,
whose purposes are pure, and whose lives are fragrant with kindness,
truthfulness, and honesty.

Alfred Barratt

In front of you lies your life. There will be many hard things to do, many a cross to carry. Christ says to you, "Take up every difficult task, every unpleasant duty, every cross; take them up one by one." You will often think that you cannot bear them. Try! Trying develops wings. The cross will turn into strong pinions that will carry you over every trouble and sorrow, over every difficulty; and by and by these same pinions will enable you to vault over the dark valley of death, and then you will awake in His likeness. Take up every duty. Trust in God. The weights will become wings and bear you heavenward.

James Learmount

When God wants to speak and deal with us, he does not avail himself of an angel but of parents, or the pastor, or of our neighbor.

Martin Luther

Paying of debts is, next to the grace of God, the best means
of delivering you from a thousand temptations to vanity and sin.

Patrick Delany

There is one case of deathbed repentance recorded,
that of the penitent thief, that none should despair;
and only one that none should presume.

St. Augustine

Of all commentaries upon the Scriptures,
good examples are the best and the liveliest.

John Donne

What matters, is not what we appear to be on the outside,
but what we have in us to become. We may seem to be very
insignificant and unattractive outwardly, but if we have the love of
Jesus in our hearts, then, although we may say, "It doth not yet
appear what we shall be," we can go on to say, as John did,
"But we know that some day we shall be like him."
J.C. Compton

Stimulate the heart to love,
and all other virtues will rise of their own accord.
W.T. Ussery

The more a person becomes irradiated with the Divinity of Christ,
the more, not the less, truly that person is human.

Phillips Brooks

Our opportunities to do good are our talents.

Cotton Mather

I never knew a child of God being bankrupted by his benevolence.
What we keep we may lose, but what we give to Christ
we are sure to keep.

Theodore L. Cuyler

Faith in tomorrow, instead of Christ,
is Satan's nurse for man's perdition.
George B. Cheever

It does not require great learning to be a Christian and be convinced
of the truth of the Bible. It requires only an honest heart
and a willingness to obey God.
Albert Barnes

You need not worry about where you yourself are.
You watch your thoughts or ideals. If your thoughts or ideals are
in the right, it will not be long before you yourself will be there,
but, on the other hand, if your thoughts or ideals are bad,
it will not be long before you will be there. If you want to be sure of
your thoughts and your ideals, all you need to do is to center them
upon Jesus Christ and what He would have you do,
and everything will be right with you.

Leslie E. Dunkin

Just think what a different world this old earth soon might become
if we imitated the flowers and took as much pleasure in comforting
the poor as in catering to the whims of the rich. And if we would live
without pride and give of our worldly possessions to satisfy the needs
of humanity; if we would obey the second great commandment given
by our Lord, "Thou shalt love thy neighbor as thyself" (*Matthew 5:43*),
then we, like flowers, could live without anxiety and die without pain.

Robert Lee Campbell

To know whom you worship, let me see you in your shop, let me
overhear you in your trade; let me know how you rent your houses,
how you get your money, how you keep it, or how it is spent.

Theodore Parker

It is as natural and reasonable for a dependent creature to apply
to its Creator for what it needs, as for a child to solicit the aid of a
parent who is believed to have the disposition
and ability to bestow what it needs.

Archibald Alexander

The Holy Spirit makes a man a Christian, and if he is a Christian
through the work of the Holy Spirit, that same spirit draws him
to other Christians in the church.
An individual Christian is no Christian at all.

R. Brokhoff

All light that does not proceed from God is false; it only dazzles us;
it sheds no illumination upon the difficult paths in which we must walk,
along the precipices that are about us.

Francois Fenelon

We have been taught the art of being strenuous,
and we have lost the art of being still.

George H. Morrison

Of all the duties enjoined by Christianity,
none is more essential, and yet more neglected, than prayer.

Francois de Salignac de La Mothe Fenelon

How sweet the name of Jesus sounds in a believer's ears!
John Newton

My religion is not vital until my heart is in it.
Christ is not a real power in my life until he gets into my heart,
for the heart is the seat of the affections.
Ralph W. Sockman

Children as soon as they can understand
ought to be told about Jesus Christ, that they may make him
the hero of their young lives.
Gerard Manley Hopkins

You may deface the image of God,
but you can never erase it.
Joseph R. Sizoo

The living Christ is not a possession to be bought,
or a commodity to exchanged.
To know him we must give ourselves to him.
Walter Dale Langtry

A man of a right spirit is not a man of narrow and private views,
but is greatly interested and concerned for the good
of the community to which he belongs, and particularly of the city
or village in which he resides, and for the true welfare
of the society of which he is a member.

Jonathan Edwards

Lay hold of the pathway which leads towards heaven;
rugged and narrow as it is, lay hold of it, and journey on.

John Chrysostom

The wind changes the atmosphere, the fire changes the temperature;
but when you have changed the atmosphere and temperature of
a soul you have accomplished a mighty transformation.

John Henry Jowett

Free will enables us to choose;
but it is grace that enables us to choose the good.

Bernard of Clairvaux

For prayer is nothing else than being on terms of friendship with God.

St. Teresa of Avila

Throughout its nature and scope, Christianity exhibits proof
of its Divine origin; and its practical precepts are no less pure
than its doctrines are sublime.
William Wilberforce

Although we cannot intrude into the mysterious dealings of God,
we can trust him to act with justice.
J. Vernon McGee

It is always easier to go with the crowd than to battle your way
against it. It is always easier to conform than to be a nonconformist.
William Barclay

Jesus has merited the title of the Great Physician
not primarily because of the specific illnesses which he cured,
but because he put the body in its proper place in the wholeness
of life. He did heal men's bodies, but he told them that if they would
seek first the kingdom of God, their bodily needs would fall
into their proper and secondary place.

Ralph W. Sockman

Let us be out and out for Christ; let us give no uncertain sound.

Dwight L. Moody

A tree has to be planted before it can spread its branches.

Theodore Parker Ferris

God never placed a Christian in a condition that he could not see
something to do, if he would but look.

W.T. Ussery

Holy and without blame we are not; holy and without blame
God may intend us to be, although we cannot or will not believe it;
but holy and without blame before him we yearn to be
with unquenchable longing—and we are never at peace until
in some measure this shall become true for us, of us, in us.

John L. Casteel

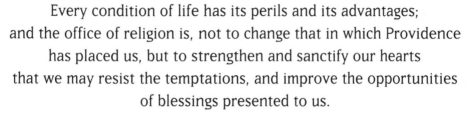

Every condition of life has its perils and its advantages;
and the office of religion is, not to change that in which Providence
has placed us, but to strengthen and sanctify our hearts
that we may resist the temptations, and improve the opportunities
of blessings presented to us.

George Washington Bethune

Trust God for great things; with your five loaves and two fishes,
He will show you a way to feed thousands.

Horace Bushnell

Carry the cross patiently, and with perfect submission;
and in the end it shall carry you.

Thomas á Kempis

Sow an act, and you reap a habit; sow a habit, and you reap a character;
sow a character, and you reap a destiny.

George Dana Boardman

The Gospel offers something to us,
but it also demands something from us.

Rolland W. Schloerb

The Lord only requires two things of us:
that we should love God and love our neighbor.

St. Teresa of Avila

It should be the lesson of our life to grow into
a holy independence of every judgment which has not the sanction
of conscience and of God.

James W. Alexander

Every step toward Christ kills a doubt. Every thought, word,
and deed for Him carries you away from discouragement.

Theodore L. Cuyler

But true Christians consider themselves as not satisfying some
rigorous creditor, but as discharging a debt of gratitude.

William Wilberforce

We must know our Bible so truly that
when we do not have it between covers we still have it.

Hampton Adams

A mighty fortress is our God, a bulwark never failing;
our helper He, amid the flood of mortal ills prevailing.

Martin Luther

Despite the weakness and triviality of many modern churches,
it is an organism, a living fellowship; the body of Christ
animated by his spirit, directed by his mind, acting as an instrument
of his loving and redeeming purpose.
David A. MacLennan

The early Christian was not called from a social unity into
"splendid isolation"; he was called into "a household of faith."
Harold A. Bosley

Thy way, not mine, O Lord, however dark it be;
lead me by thine own hand; choose out the path for me.
Horatius Bonar

Outside the church is no truth, no Christ, no blessedness.
Martin Luther

Too many persons seem to use their religion as a diver does his bell,
to venture down into the depths of worldliness with safety,
and there grope for pearls, with just so much of heaven's air as will
keep them from suffocating, and no more; and some, alas! as at times
is the case with the diver, are suffocated in the experiment.
George B. Cheever

All my theology is reduced to this narrow compass,
"Jesus Christ came into the world to save sinners."
Archibald Alexander

I heard a man on television say that
only one New Testament Scripture speaks of restoration.
My question for him is "How many references does it take?"
Don Crossland

Every generation needs to rethink, restate, and creatively apply
its theological heritage to its own situation.
In this way the heritage stays vital, and relevant.
Mildred Bangs Wynkoop

Let us, then, attach ourselves to those who are religiously
devoted to peace, and not to those who are for it hypocritically.

Clement of Rome

No man can have God as his Father
who has not the church as his Mother.

John Calvin

There is no such thing as a solitary Christian.

John Wesley

The injuries of life, if rightly improved, will be to us as the strokes of
the statuary on his marble, forming us to a more beautiful shape,
and making us fitter to adorn the heavenly temple.
Cotton Mather

Prayer is the wing wherewith the soul flies to heaven,
and meditation the eye wherewith we see God.
Ambrose of Milan

If there be ground for you to trust in your own righteousness, then,
all that Christ did to purchase salvation,
and all that God did to prepare the way for it is in vain.
Jonathan Edwards

Science is beginning to catch up with Jesus in his understanding
of the role of faith, hope, and love in the cure of disease
and the maintenance of health.

Albert Edward Day

We do not always come through our testings as we wish we would.
Yet time after time we are brought back to our tasks
with renewed determination because of the trust our Lord puts in us.
And always we seem to feel the assurance that through him
the victory will be won.

Gerald Kennedy

God reaches in two directions:
He reaches down and He reaches out.
Ralph A. Herring

But deep within ourselves, if we persevere in patience and fidelity,
we will again and again be given some intimation of the work
God is bringing to pass in us: the restoration of the clean heart,
the recreation of the right spirit, and the secret growth of his own
divine beauty and righteousness within us. And we shall be amazed
at his grace, and shall find ourselves possessed of joy
which passes understanding.
John L. Casteel

We have not only to be called Christians, but to be Christians.
Ignatius of Antioch

The best advertisement of a workshop is firstclass work.
The strongest attraction to Christianity is a wellmade Christian character.
Theodore L. Cuyler

The remedy for the present threatened decay of faith
is not a more stalwart creed or a more unflinching acceptance of it,
but a profoundly spiritual life.
Lyman Abbott

Serve God in fear and in truth, forsaking empty talkativeness
and the erroneous teaching of the crowd.

Polycarp of Smyrna

It is not too much to say that, second only to faith in God,
our human relationships are the most important thing in our lives.

Samuel M. Shoemaker

As a man goes down in self, he goes up in God.

George B. Cheever

A man's neighbor is everyone who needs help.
Cunningham Geikie

Regardless of the terms in which equality may be debated
in other arenas, Christianity proposes to ignore the relative
historical achievements and standards of people to raise everyone
into the equality of fellowship as children of God.
Duke K. McCall

Easter is the story of a discovery, the discovery that Christ lives.
He is alive in the world. It has taken one deep fear out of life,
the fear of death.
Joseph R. Sizoo

A tender conscience is an inestimable blessing; that is,
a conscience not only quick to discern what is evil,
but instantly to shun it, as the eyelid closes itself against the mote.
Nehemiah Adams

God is the God of truth;
and every spiritual quality must live with that holy attribute.
Edwin Holt Hughes

Every man's life is a plan of God.
Horace Bushnell

He that lives to live forever, never fears dying.
William Penn

No disciple who aspires to a vigorous spiritual life
can afford to neglect the Bible.
Clovis G. Chappell

The greatest thing of all in giving pleasure to God is love.
It is impossible to please Him unless there be some knowledge
of His love in our hearts and some love to Him in return.
G.B.F. Hallock

It is better to remember life than death. And best of all is it to live with Christ every day. That is the best preparation for immortal life.

James Learmount

A little while ago a Sunday school teacher in the last stage of rapid consumption was asked by a friend who visited her, "Are you afraid to die?" "I am not going to die," was her cheerful reply as she pointed to the motto that hung upon the wall of her chamber which read, "The gift of God is eternal life." She believed that those words were true, and so she knew and was confident that for her there was no death. It is Jesus who died. And because He has died and risen again we need never die.

Alfred Barratt

Big purposes free us from petty fretfulness and little ailments.

Ralph W. Sockman

Grant that I may not pray alone with the mouth;
help me that I may pray from the depths of my heart.

Martin Luther

Grant me no more than to be a sacrifice for God.

Ignatius of Antioch

Grace is but glory begun, and glory is but grace perfected.
Jonathan Edwards

How blessed and amazing are God's gifts, dear friends!
Life with immortality, splendor with righteousness,
truth with confidence, faith with assurance, self-control with holiness!
And all these things are within our comprehension.
Clement of Rome

The Lord gets His best soldiers out of the highlands of affliction.
Charles Haddon Spurgeon

The heart that is to be filled to the brim with holy joy
must be held still.
George Seaton Bowes

Live as with God; and whatever be your calling,
pray for the gift that will perfectly qualify you in it.
Horace Bushnell

Christian evangelism is not a call to occupy the rocking chair of grace
for the rest of one's natural—or unnatural—life.
It is a challenge to take to the road in the discipleship of Him
who will be forever on the road until the last person
and the last area of human life are redeemed.
Albert Edward Day

It is a truism that if you permit others to do the things that in reality
are yours to do, you will soon be obliged to do as these others say
you must do. Difficulty develops. Work makes one strong.
Laziness, shirking makes one weak. We learn to bear responsibility
by bearing responsibility. There are benefits in service.
G.B.F. Hallock

A church in prevailing prayer is a church in prevailing power.
W.T. Ussery

All that Jesus does for us reflects only a small part of his concern
in comparison with that which he desires to do through us.
Ralph A. Herring

The holiest of men still need Christ as their King, for God does not
give them a stock of holiness. But unless they receive a supply
each moment, nothing but unholiness would remain.
Even perfect holiness is acceptable to God only through Jesus Christ.
John Wesley

Humility, a blessed grace, smooths the furrows of care,
and gilds the dark paths of life. It will make us kind, tenderhearted,
affable, and enable us to do more for God and the gospel
than the most fervent zeal without it.

Henry Martyn

Nothing you can see has real value. Our God Jesus Christ, indeed,
has revealed himself more clearly by returning to the Father.
Ignatius of Antioch

Resignation and faith behold God in the smallest hair that falls;
and the happiest life is that of him who has bound together
all the affairs of life, great and small, and entrusted them to God.
James W. Alexander

The Holy Spirit is a centrifugal force that attracts believers
into churches. The power of the Spirit is a divine magnet
which draws all men to Christ and to each other.

R. Brokhoff

Family education and order are some of the chief means of grace;
if these are duly maintained, all the means of grace
are likely to prosper and become effectual.

Jonathan Edwards

Few people are ever "successful" as the world sees success unless
they know how to get along with other people; and many fail,
in the worldly sense and in the Christian sense also, because they do not.

Samuel M. Shoemaker

People who seek God do not poke and putter in the muck and mire
of the world; they lift their eyes unto the heavens.
Duke K. McCall

Christ gives us patience and fortitude to endure the things that
cannot be changed. But he also came to give us courage to challenge
the things which should be changed—and wisdom to know the difference.
Ralph W. Sockman

Stop thinking about your difficulties, whatever they are,
and start thinking about God instead.
Emmet Fox

To those whom He counts worthy, Christ gives the gift of suffering—
not as a strange thing—but as a badge of honor,
that we wear proudly in His name.
Bernard Iddings Bell

The primary task of the Church is not to mend the manners
of the community, but to proclaim the matchless gospel of
the Lord Jesus Christ. When people hear that gospel and believe it,
their lives will give evidence of their faith.
Walter Dale Langtry

Do not talk Jesus Christ and set your heart on the world.
Ignatius of Antioch

Life was not planned to be a perpetual picnic for children
but a school for adult education.
Herbert Welch

When James writes in his epistle, "purify your hearts" (4:8),
the Greek wording shows a passive verb which indicates that the
purifying is done to us. We can't purify our own hearts.
God has to do this, but we can put ourselves in the position
to be purified by God.
Don Crossland

Virtue consists in doing our duty in the various relations
we sustain to ourselves, to our fellowmen, and to God,
as it is made known by reason, revelation, and Providence.
Archibald Alexander

On this side of the grave we are exiles, on that, citizens;
on this side, orphans, on that, children; on this side, captives,
on that, freemen; on this side disguised, unknown,
on that, disclosed and proclaimed as the sons of God.
Henry Ward Beecher

The best and noblest lives are those which are set toward high ideals.
And the highest and noblest ideal that anyone can have
is Jesus of Nazareth.

René Almeron

We are all in the hands of an omnipotent, omniscient,
just and merciful God, and whatever may be the destiny of humanity
(for weal or woe), there will be a universal and eternal amen
to all that God does.

W.T. Ussery

Christ is not valued at all unless He is valued above all.

St. Augustine

Knowledge is vain and fruitless which is not reduced to practice.
Matthew Henry

It is one of the anomalies of our day that, while civilization trembles
at the possibility of destruction, the American people spend more
time than ever laughing themselves to death. While hospitals are
crowded with nervous and mental wrecks; while suicide, crime,
broken homes, and delinquency set records, television clowns are
paid fortunes to amuse us night after night, turning tragedy
into comedy. Never in history has there been more ribald hilarity
with less to be funny about. Unfortunately, this attitude
has spilled over into the church.
Vance Havner

Words of Peace, Wisdom, and Encouragement from Fellow Believers

A house is made to be lived in and not to be lived for.
Ralph W. Sockman

In the midst of our ordinary affairs God breaks in upon us
and we learn, sooner or later, that the most inexorable fact of our life
is simply that he is never going to leave us alone.
John L. Casteel

God hath promised pardon to him that repenteth,
but he hath not promised repentance to him that sinneth.
St. Anselm

Resolve to live as with all your might while you do live,
and as you shall wish you had done ten thousand years hence.
Jonathan Edwards

If honor be your clothing, the suit will last a lifetime;
but if clothing be your honor, it will soon be worn threadbare.
William D. Arnot

I am faithful to the duties of the present,
God will provide for the future.
Gregory T. Bedell

None but a theology that came out of eternity
can carry you and me safely to and through eternity.

Theodore L. Cuyler

To endure the cross is not tragedy; it is suffering which is the fruit of
an exclusive allegiance to Jesus Christ.

Dietrich Bonhoeffer

Temptation always looks desirable to the one tempted.
Otherwise it would not be a temptation.
But sin does not turn out as good as it looks. It turns out very bad.

G.B.F. Hallock

When an affluent society would coax us to believe that happiness
consists in the size of our automobiles, the impressiveness
of our houses, and the expensiveness of our clothes,
Jesus reminds us, "A man's life consisteth not in the abundance
of the things which he possesseth."

Martin Luther King

Prayer opens the heart to God,
and it is the means by which the soul, though empty, is filled by God.

John Bunyan

The world is dying for want, not of good preaching,
but of good hearing.
George Dana Boardman

All unbelief is the belief of a lie.
Horatius Bonar

Every dollar dedicated to God and His cause glorifies Him
and strengthens His Kingdom.
W.T. Ussery

The world is saying to the Church today:
We are sick and tired of listening to your debates and quarrels,
and your ecclesiastical contentions. We would see Jesus.
G. Campbell Morgan

The New Testament makes it abundantly clear
that whenever the Kingdom of God was concerned Jesus was
absolutely uncompromising, even when he realized that for him
personally the alternative to compromise was crucifixion.
Ernest Fremont Tittle

Faith comes by hearing the word of God. The church teaches and
preaches the word of God. As people hear it with open minds
and hearts, the Holy Spirit enters and creates this saving faith.

R. Brokhoff

Small deeds done are better than great deeds planned.

Peter Marshall

Do we demonstrate before the world what we confess?
Is there anything about us and our movement that the world
cannot explain away, about which it must say God is at work?

Leighton Ford

Whatever we ask of God, let us also work toward it,
if there is anything we can do.
Jeremy Taylor

Plain horse sense ought to tell us that anything that makes no change
in the one who professes it makes no difference to God, either.
A.W. Tozer

Obedience means marching right on, whether we feel it or not.
D.L. Moody

I will set no value on anything I have or may possess
except in relation to the Kingdom of God.
David Livingstone

The fewer the words, the better the prayer.
Martin Luther

It is a little thing to trust God as far as we can see Him, so far as
the way lies open before us; but to trust in Him when we are
hedged in on every side and can see no way to escape,
this is good and acceptable with God.
John Wesley

Words of Peace, Wisdom, and Encouragement from Fellow Believers

The problem of unholy living does not stem from the fact
that we desire to use money and time unwisely; the problem is
that we do not intend to be as responsible and devout as we can.
William Law

The affections of the Godly are the same to everyone.
Bernard of Clairvaux

God never gave a man a thing to do, concerning which it were
irreverent to ponder how the Son of God would have done it.
George MacDonald